Portrait of Cancer

An Artist's Journey
Through Breast Cancer

Written and Illustrated by

Parson's Porch Books

Portrait of Cancer: An Artist's Journey Through Breast Cancer

ISBN: Softcover 978-1-951472-70-2

Copyright © 2020 by Ruth Wilgus Gehring

www.parsonsporch.com

DEDICATION

For Martin, William, and Allison,
whose love sustained me all along the way.

INTRODUCTION

In addition to my family members and friends who supported me with such love, this is for all of the members of the "Club Nobody Wants to Join". It is for the breast cancer survivors who live as broken, scarred, exploding stars shining a light for others. And it is for those currently in the midst of this tough journey of their own. May it bring light to the darkness and strength to those who need it.

DIAGNOSIS AND TESTING PHASE:
11/27/18-12/18/18

December, 2018

CANCER: a word I have feared my whole life now defines and absorbs my very being. I'm now a statistic. I'm now desperately praying to end up as one of the good statistics.

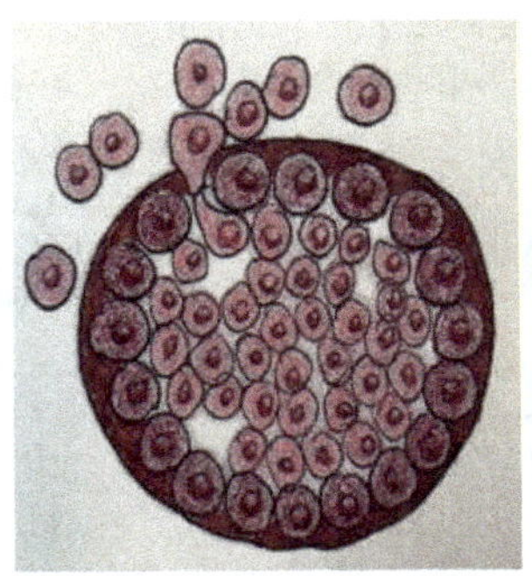

Thoughts of this word first began the middle of September, 2018, mere weeks prior to a move from Richmond, Michigan to Columbus, Ohio. During a routine self-exam of my breasts I felt a lump. I've had lumps come and go over the years, so in the chaos of packing for the move, I had no other thought than to keep an eye on it.

We moved during the first week of October, followed by a flurry of unpacking, arranging furniture and hanging pictures. But as I kept checking the lump, I realized that something felt different. I looked back through the calendar to remember when I had my last mammogram and saw that my 3-D digital imaging had just been done in January with a normal result. Since insurance only covers one mammogram per year, I opted to continue monitoring it.

By mid-November it felt more prominent and was really nagging my conscience. I made an appointment with a new doctor for a physical, November 27, just after Thanksgiving. I knew I would need a doctor to order a mammogram in order to bypass the insurance rule. Upon examination, my new doctor shared my concern and also pointed out another suspicious area that I had not noticed. With his request I could have gotten in for diagnostic imaging the very next day if it were not for our recent move. I had to put in a request for my previous imaging to be sent to them first. Now, why is it that a digital image can't be sent with the click of a button? For whatever reason, it caused me to wait another eight days for my diagnostic mammogram appointment.

I knew that I might very likely go straight from mammography to ultrasound imaging, but I began to have a sinking feeling when the ultrasound technician got quieter. Then came the feeling of dread when the doctor was called in to look at the images; then a feeling of fear when they took me down the hall to get me squeezed into the schedule of the cancer surgeon (who my new general practice doctor had already selected for me); then a feeling of abject terror when the physician's assistant went through the explanation of the likelihood that this was indeed cancer and what steps would take place next.

The very next day I was back in for needle biopsies of the 2 suspect areas as well as an enlarged lymph node. The numbing shots hurt like hell, with one of them hitting a vein or capillary causing blood to spurt into the air and onto the doctor's shirt. (I'm guessing she was thinking she should have worn a lab coat at that moment.) All of the nurses were so kind and gentle with me through all of this. Swollen and bruised from the needle biopsies, I tried to come to terms with the probability that my results would show cancer.

So that's the backstory of my confirmation of breast cancer, received via phone call December 10, 2018. I'm calm in my voice, yet screaming inside my head during this call. I feel weak in the knees as the schedule of next steps is explained and set in motion: an MRI (for finer tuned imaging of the tumor or tumors and lymph nodes), followed by a CT scan and bone scan. I call my husband, Martin, who comes home from work immediately. I tearfully text my son and daughter, both of whom already live in Columbus, and get messages to other family members. I'm sobbing, afraid, and feel such guilt that I didn't get moving on this sooner. I have never felt such paralyzing fear.

The barrage of tests, and the rapidity with which they are done, frightens me even more. My diagnosis is stage 3 invasive ductal carcinoma with estrogen, progesterone, and Her-2 positive characteristics: foreign words which will become part of my everyday vocabulary for the next year. I'm told that being triple positive is not as bad as it sounds due to the number of chemical treatments to which it will respond. OK, still sounds freakishly scary to me. And how can I have gotten to stage 3 in only eleven months from a normal mammogram? It is explained to me that Her-2 is a protein which attaches to cancer cells, making them grow at an accelerated rate. Stage 3 invasive means that the mass is not small and has invaded the lymph nodes. I'm scared.

So now it's time for all of that frightening further testing. The MRI reveals my tumor to be 2 connected areas of mass, 11cm in size, present in 3 lymph nodes near my under arm, as well as 1 node under the sternum. The CT scan and bone scan will determine if the cancer has spread to my organs or bones. With all of the crying I have done in the short time of processing this, I cry the hardest with a sense of relief when I get the call that it has not spread further. Knowing that this could have been much worse, I try to feel thankful for any good news that I receive. I also have genetic testing done, which will determine if I have to consider a bilateral mastectomy as

a precaution. Thankfully, all genetic markers are negative. This relieves me of concern for the risk factors for my son and daughter, as well as eliminating the need for a bilateral mastectomy.

My treatment plan, as explained by my surgeon, is daunting and overwhelming: chemotherapy, recovery, mastectomy, recovery, radiation, recovery, reconstructive surgery, recovery, all while spending the entire year receiving drugs to combat the Her-2 protein. For a year of my life I will be battling a monster that wants to kill me!! It's so frightening that I can scarcely comprehend it. A **whole year** dedicated to fighting my biggest fear, with no certainty of the outcome.

In my initial consultation with my oncologist one week prior to Christmas, I'm given the option of waiting until after the holidays to begin my first phase of treatment. My answer: NO!! Now that I know how fast this is spreading, I don't want to give it a chance to go further. So, Phase 1 of my treatment plan will begin 4 days before Christmas. Every 3 weeks, for 6 rounds, I will have infusions of 2 chemotherapy drugs (Taxotere and Carboplatin) as well as 2 targeted therapy drugs (Herseptin and Perjeta) aimed at turning off the signals of the Her-2 receptor. The second 2 drugs I will continue receiving every 3 weeks for the full year. It seems overwhelming. Merry Christmas to me.

Now I have to gear up for the fight of my life. The fight **for** my life. I gather as much information as I can for my weaponry. My surgeon arms me with a breast cancer treatment handbook that is a comprehensive guide, the equivalent of a textbook full of excellent information. My oncologist arms me with a 3-ring binder full of information on my specific drugs, all of the possible side effects, and management of those side effects. My nurse navigator arms me with brochures on nutrition during chemotherapy, information on shops that sell hats and wigs, and more information about all of the free services available to cancer patients in my area. This is a lot of reading! But am I going to be able to take on this fight, this battle, this war?

Am I brave enough? Am I strong enough?

My husband, Martin, is a pastor and a very supportive, caring, and insightful person. He helped re-frame my thinking a bit by saying that I should look at this as a "Journey to Recovery" rather than a battle. Somehow that idea brings a small measure of calm with it. So now I begin the Journey. It will not be easy, and there will be a lot of rocky terrain ahead. Nevertheless, into the wilderness I now forge ahead, with his loving assurance that I'm strong and able to make it through to the end.

PHASE 1: CHEMOTHERAPY
12/21/18-04/05/19

December 2018

On "Chemo Eve" we decide to have a celebration night to kick off the start of the journey. A night of getting dressed up, going out for a special evening, and drinking a toast to whatever is to come. As it turns out, about a month or so ago we had already purchased tickets for this night to see a performance of "The Nutcracker" ballet. I put on a nice dress, pretty shoes and sparkly jewelry, then get out the good stemware for our celebratory toasts. We take photos and feel glamorous as we enjoy our evening.

Despite the happy evening, I sleep fitfully and wake up feeling nervous and frightened in the early morning quiet. Even with all of the information I have been given, I really don't know what to expect. Will chemotherapy hurt? Will I feel sick or throw up? I'm in a bit of a panic, so I do some visualizing. I try to come up with an image of some sort of spirit creature I can rely on to do battle with the beast inside my body. I'm not very successful at coming up with anything and remind myself of the thought of journey-instead-of-fight. But the only terrain that comes to mind is either extremely rough, rocky, and rugged, or is very dark and scary. Clearly, I'm not helping my anxiety with this exercise in visualization. Maybe I'll get better with time and practice.

Instead, I say some prayers. I pray for stamina. I pray for strength. I pray for an easing of my fears about this first treatment day. Mostly I pray that I will ultimately survive this journey. Please, God, let me survive this!

I get up to have a light breakfast, but no coffee as per my oncologist's instructions. (Caffeine restricts the veins, making it harder to insert the IV. Stupid IV.) I drink a lot of water, also per instructions, but cannot make myself eat much. I'm too nervous and afraid of feeling sick.

I am to be there by 8:00am, and expect to be there for several hours. Knowing it will be a long day, I bring along a bag of distractions: a book to read, Sudoku puzzles, and a few scrapbook pages ready to assemble for a Christmas present project. Martin comes along to endure the day-long treatment schedule. The poor guy will have to spend the day in an uncomfortable chair while I will at least be in a recliner. But I'm thankful not to face this day alone.

After checking in, I first go to the lab for a blood draw. They will do this each time to check specifics of my blood. Then I see my oncologist. He explains to me that my particular drugs, given once every 3 weeks, will have a downward arc as to how I feel. I'm told I won't feel too bad for the first week, will feel worse when I hit my low blood count week, then will start feeling better in week three before the whole cycle begins again. I will also be taking steroids and super strong anti-nausea pills the day before, day of, and two days after each chemo infusion. I'm very thankful that he is so forthcoming with information, but also grateful for his calm and caring demeanor. I feel that I'm in good hands.

Next, I move on to the infusion room. A very friendly and kind nurse helps me get set up in a large recliner with an attached table tray and a side table. I get all of my things set up on the side table: water bottle, cell phone and charger, reading glasses, pen and pencil, and my previously mentioned distractions. Then comes the insertion of the IV, and **OUCH!!!** that hurts going in! (My oncologist feels that having a port is too much of an infection risk and only uses them as a last resort.) I feel the cold saline going in first, into which I am given some

anti-anxiety medicine, and it begins. One medicine at a time drips through the IV, separated by "observation" time and more saline. As if I hadn't been poked enough, at the end of the afternoon a device is adhered to my abdomen with a timer to automatically administer a shot 24 hours after chemo. We schedule the next appointment and go home.

I begin to experience some side effects within hours of leaving my appointment. First, diarrhea. That's not fun. Second, extreme fatigue. I start to feel tired while Martin is fixing dinner and fall asleep on the couch shortly after eating. But I don't feel nearly as awful as I might have expected. With Christmas only a few days away, I'm thankful for that, at least.

Christmas is bittersweet. Cancer's presence is palpable, a physical reminder of my own mortality, following my every step. Will I still be here next Christmas? I want to drink in every moment and savor it, just in case. I keep on a brave face, a graceful presence, a celebratory smile. It's our first Christmas in our new church and our new home. It's the first time in several years that we live in the same town as our grown son and daughter. I want to turn to that dark entity of cancer following my footsteps and, quoting Ripley in the movie "Aliens," say, "Get away from her, you bitch!" But I also don't want to feel anger, sadness, or grief at this joyous time of the year. I only want to feel love. And I do. And, mercifully, time slows down enough for me to savor the moments with my family.

My sister, Barbara, arrives the day after Christmas for a brief visit with me before traveling on for my extended family's annual gathering in Chattanooga, Tennessee. I will not be able to attend that gathering this year because I'm just about to hit my first low-ebb low-blood-count phase and it's a very long drive. Not being able to see all of my family saddens me greatly.

Knowing that I can expect hair loss to begin in 3-5 weeks, Barbara and I go to a salon to get my shoulder length hair cut shorter. I'm not quite able to muster the courage to go super short with it and opt for a shortish bob. It will be less messy than longer hair when it begins to fall out. My sister is a good source of cheer and support during her short visit.

Though my new sassy hairstyle looks cute, I know it won't last and am already grieving the loss of my hair even before it's gone. First of all, having grown up with lovely auburn red hair, my hair was always a part of my identity. And even though my red hair was

graying, it was still beautiful. My friends said it looked more blond than gray. Redheads don't gray in a salt-and-pepper manner, but in more of a cinnamon-and-sugar or copper-and-silver way. Secondly, women's images of beauty and self-esteem are often centered around their hair. I don't know how I will handle it.

January 2019

I don't make it past 3 weeks before hair loss begins. It's so sudden! At first, more hairs than usual are in the hairbrush or on my shoulders or pillow. Then, on January 9, big handfuls come out in the shower. The cancer center where I did all of my diagnostic testing offers a free service of head shaving. With tears in my eyes, and a very shaky voice, I call to make an appointment. They say the barber can meet me there in the afternoon. Martin leaves work to offer support. I begin to cry with the first swipe of the shaver. He cuts it super short but doesn't feel I need it shaved all the way. I'm

grateful, but I don't look like myself anymore. As we leave I buy a soft cotton hat to add to the several hats and scarves lovingly sent to me by friends. Even though my hair isn't completely gone, my head feels cold.

January 20 it becomes clear that my "Jamie Lee Curtis" style haircut isn't going to last. It's time to let it go. Martin lovingly and

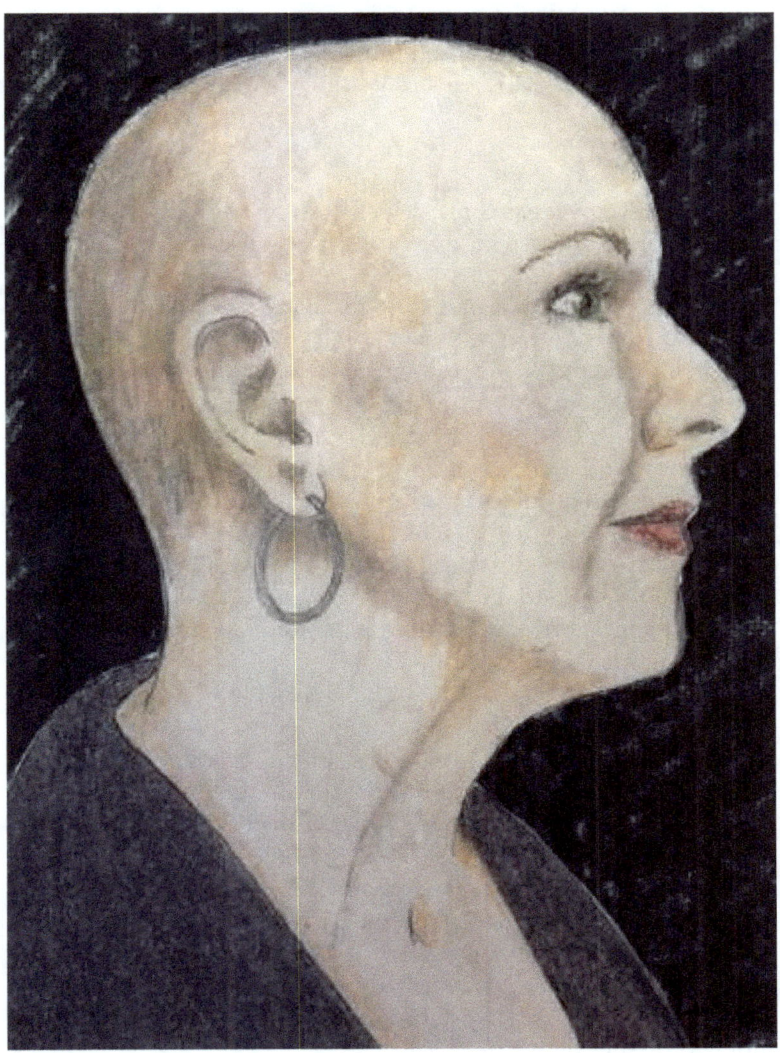

carefully shaves my head with his electric razor. I hold a towel over my face to prevent little hairs from falling in my eyes, and silently weep. He holds me close and lets me cry when the job is completed. He tells me he loves me, but I'm unable to speak. I can't look him in the eyes. I go upstairs to shower and can't bear to look in the mirror until afterwards. Then I weep some more, put on a soft hat, put on some makeup and a brave face, and return downstairs to look my amazing, wonderful husband in the face. Those vows of "for better or for worse, in sickness and in health" have never really been tested before. Our relationship is strong and can withstand this, God willing.

February 2019

Chemotherapy treatments, which I know will get tougher as it accumulates in my system, have at least begun to be predictable in their side effects:

1) The steroids are beginning to make my face puffy.

2) The super strong anti-nausea pill that I take for 4 days the weekend of chemo leaves me feeling fuzzy-headed. By day 3 my hands are shaky and my skin hurts. I don't like it at all.

3) By exactly day 8 after my infusion, the nausea enters the picture for a few days. I'm taking my regular strength anti-nausea pill preemptively each day of that second weekend and then just as needed.

4) I have strong heartburn, especially after eating anything but small portions of food. I'm taking a daily antacid pill to combat this and eating small portions of food at more frequent intervals. I'm also avoiding all spicy food.

5) All food now tastes bland or has a metallic aftertaste. I haven't really developed any particular food aversions, just a vague indifference as nothing really has much flavor. It all tastes disappointing to me unless it's very salty or very sour, which isn't healthy. I now just eat for nutrition rather than for pleasure.

6) Though not on a predictable schedule, I have diarrhea 3-4 times a week. It's gross and my rear end is irritated and tender. I take anti-diarrhea medicine along with me wherever I go.

7) Another thing that's not on a predictable schedule are the nosebleeds. My nose runs constantly, perhaps due to even my nose hairs dropping out. At least once a week it bleeds. I have a constant supply of tissues on hand.

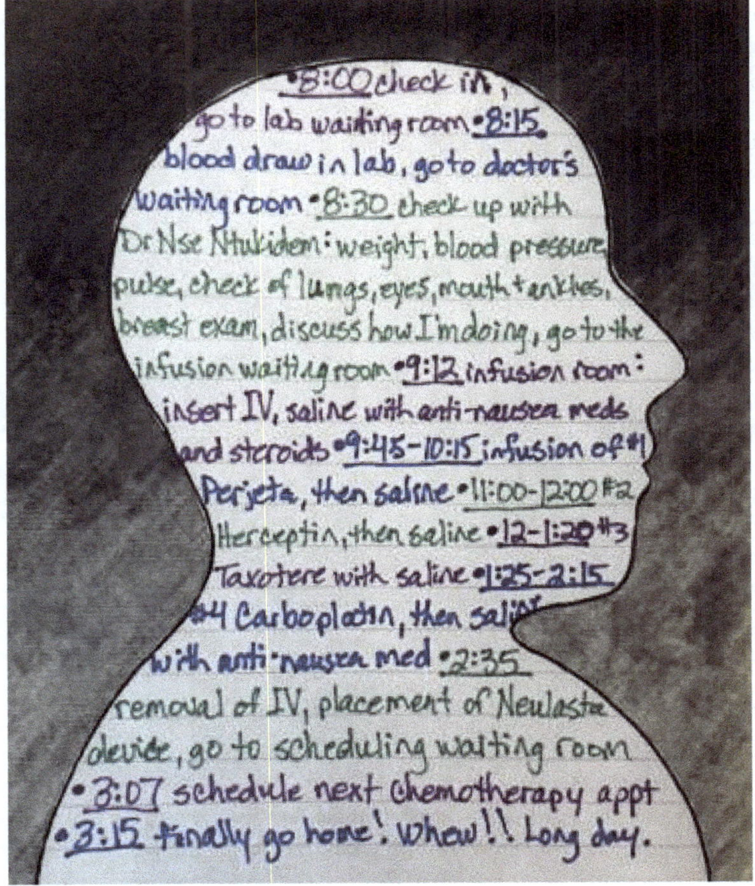

8) Fatigue is a constant the weekend of chemo and during my low-ebb week. I nap frequently and adhere to a strict bedtime routine.

9) Each time I have chemotherapy, the skin along the vein in which the IV was placed becomes itchy and red within a few days of the infusion. I'm using hydrocortisone cream to help.

The good news is that I'm now, as of February 8, halfway through my chemotherapy treatments. I have to look at the positive points whenever I can. Another positive aspect in all of this awfulness is how kind people are being. I am sent a lap quilt from women at our former church and a soft prayer shawl from a knitting group at our current church. People also regularly provide food for us. I receive thoughtful cards, gifts, and flowers from many friends. I'm truly and deeply touched by all of this. It is wonderful how much organized support is out there for cancer patients!

One dear friend, who comes to sit with me for a couple of hours during my infusions, gives me a beautiful soft leather-bound journal which I now use to artistically process my journey. I have a second journal in which I am illustrating quotes that have meaning for me. These are my personal art therapy projects, which are helping my thoughts to remain positive. Although my background is in art, I have worked as a preschool teacher from 2001 until just before our move. For quite some time I haven't been using my artistic skills as often as I would have liked. It feels refreshing and empowering just to be doing art again. It brings some joy and light into the darkness of this journey.

March 2019

The previously mentioned side effects remain a constant in my life. Some have gotten stronger. I'm feeling much more tired as the chemo drugs accumulate in my system. The vein reactions have gotten worse and look awful. My eyes have begun watering a lot. Up until now, I have somehow kept my eyelashes and eyebrows. Now they are coming out too, which probably explains the watery eyes. I'm frequently dabbing at my eyes while explaining that I'm not crying. It makes singing in choir challenging when my eyes fill with tears and blur the music. How annoying!

I'm also struggling a bit with self-image. The loss of hair, and now eyelashes and brows, combined with the steroid puffy face make me feel ugly. I do a decent job with makeup, hats, and scarves to look the best I can, but I don't look like me. I find that I'm frequently avoiding eye contact with people. I've been doing self-portraits in my small leather journal. Believe me, this is not out of vanity! Rather, it is a way of processing and coming to terms with my changing self-image. By drawing myself, I'm forced to really look at my face as it is now. More changes in my body will come with Phase 2 of my journey, so I may as well get used to change.

April 2019

My final chemotherapy treatment is on April 5th. Goodbye and good riddance to those poisons! Although I'm happy about that, it doesn't feel completed. After all, I will still be coming in and sitting in the recliner with an IV hooked to my arm every 3 weeks for the remainder of the year for the Her-2 targeted drugs. But it does mean that some of my worst side effects will begin to fade. And it also means that my time in the infusion room will reduce from 6-7 hours to 2-3 hours. So it's definitely a noteworthy moment and milestone. Phase 1 is done; recovery time and preparation for Phase 2 begin!

My post-chemo MRI brings excellent news: my body has

responded well to the medicines and shows no signs of active cancer! However, this doesn't mean I can skip all of the next parts of my treatment plan. Cancer is an elusive beast that can hide, deceive, resurrect itself and ambush. It seems it's not the time for confetti and champagne yet.

I continue with all of the next steps in the recovery time period. I have my next echo-cardiogram-- these are necessary quarterly due to the possibility of Herseptin temporarily weakening my heart. I do regular cardio health exercises to prevent this side effect. Other next steps include consultations with the surgeons. I'm pleased to learn that I have the option of simultaneous reconstructive surgery using my own body tissues at the time of the mastectomy. For now, I just need recovery time.

May 2019

My surgery date is set for June 3rd with a follow up outpatient surgery on June 10th. The month of May is full of pre-op appointments. Because micro-vascular surgery will be involved in the reconstruction, I first have to get a more detailed CT scan. Then there is the pre-op blood work and an EKG with my primary care doctor.

I'm realizing that the timing of my surgeries is going to prevent me from attending my niece's wedding in Georgia this June. This breaks my heart, as it is the first of our nieces and nephews to get married. Plus, I already had to miss out on my family's post-Christmas annual gathering. So I take a window in between May appointments and travel south to see at least part of the family for a few days, including my niece.

The month ends with a final consultation with the plastic surgeons who will be doing the Deep Inferior Perferator (DIEP) flap reconstruction. It will be quite a choreographed dance in the operating room. While my cancer surgeon performs the mastectomy and lymph node testing on my left breast, a team of 2 micro-vascular reconstructive plastic surgeons will be removing tissue from my abdomen. (Yes, I will end up getting a tummy tuck out of this ordeal – at least a bit of a silver lining!) Once the mastectomy is finished, that surgeon will leave while the 2 plastic surgeons work on putting me back together, replacing my lost breast with one created from my tummy tissue. Altogether, the surgery will take 5-6 hours.

I like my team of doctors. I trust them and have complete

confidence in them. Yet, it is still major, invasive surgery. I cannot pretend that I'm not nervous. In fact, I'm downright scared. I've never had major surgery, much less such intensely invasive surgery. That dark entity begins to look over my shoulder again, reminding me once more that mortality is not in my control. I schedule a therapeutic massage appointment (one of the perks of my treatment center) to try and calm my nerves. It's time to get my game face on. Time to summon my Holy Brave from the depths of my fear.

PHASE 2: SURGERY
6/3/19 AND 6/10/19

June 2019

We decide to kick off each phase with another Celebration Night. This time we schedule a night out a couple of days in advance, due to not being allowed any "adult beverages" within 48 hours prior to surgery. We have a gift card to a nice restaurant, which sounds perfect for our celebratory toasts. Since we get lucky with a warm evening filled with golden sun, we opt to dine in the outdoor patio area. I feel self-conscious with my head tied in a scarf while we are surrounded by young, hip, good-looking people. But Martin keeps me focused on our purpose for the evening and raises his glass to my beauty and bravery. He's the best.

The morning of surgery I'm allowed a little water, but nothing else. I'm sleep deprived because of nervousness and fearful thoughts. Martin and our daughter, Allison, are with me in the pre-op room where I'm greeted by nurses (who gather all of my information and prep me with IVs and a blood pressure cuff), my cancer surgeon and one of the plastic surgeons (who reassure me and ask if I have any more questions of them), and the anesthesiologist (who chats with me about what to expect before sending Martin and Allison out to the waiting area). My eyes well up with tears after I watch them walk away from the prep room. OK. Deep breath. This is it.

My first post-surgery memory is of "surfacing" with moans and frowns and a feeling of intense pain in my abdominal area. I'm guessing they give me more pain medication, because my next memory is seeing Martin, Allison, and our son, William, in my hospital room smiling at me. I see the worried eyes that accompany the smiles and guess that I don't look so good. It was a lengthy procedure, after all. The abdominal pain is under control and now the breast pain comes into my awareness. I can't move much, which is just as well since I have all kinds of things attached to me.

I get my first look at my incision areas later in the evening when dressings are changed. It looks less scary than I imagined it would, though quite bruised. I have stitches from hip to hip, around my belly button, and around a circular area of the newly created breast. I have 2 drain tubes ending in a collection bulb coming out of the side of my left breast and 2 more coming from either end of the abdominal incision. The drain amounts are emptied and measured periodically.

I'm told the surgeons kept my family informed during my surgery. I see each of the surgeons over the 4-day stay during their daily rounds, and feel very lucky to have ended up with such a good medical team.

The days in the hospital are monotonous, but necessary. The nights are fragmented, punctuated by nurse visits – also necessary. Sitting up in a chair feels good, yet surprisingly tiring. Walking is challenging. I have to roll the IV pole along with me; and can't yet stand up straight. Having stretched the skin to cover what was removed for the new breast leaves my belly feeling tight and tender. I'm told it takes about 2 weeks before I can stand fully straight. I walk extremely slowly.

On the fourth day, as Martin and I await our care instructions and training on emptying and measuring drainage from the drain tubes, I receive a very welcome call from my cancer surgeon. She lets me know the pathology of the removed lymph nodes and breast

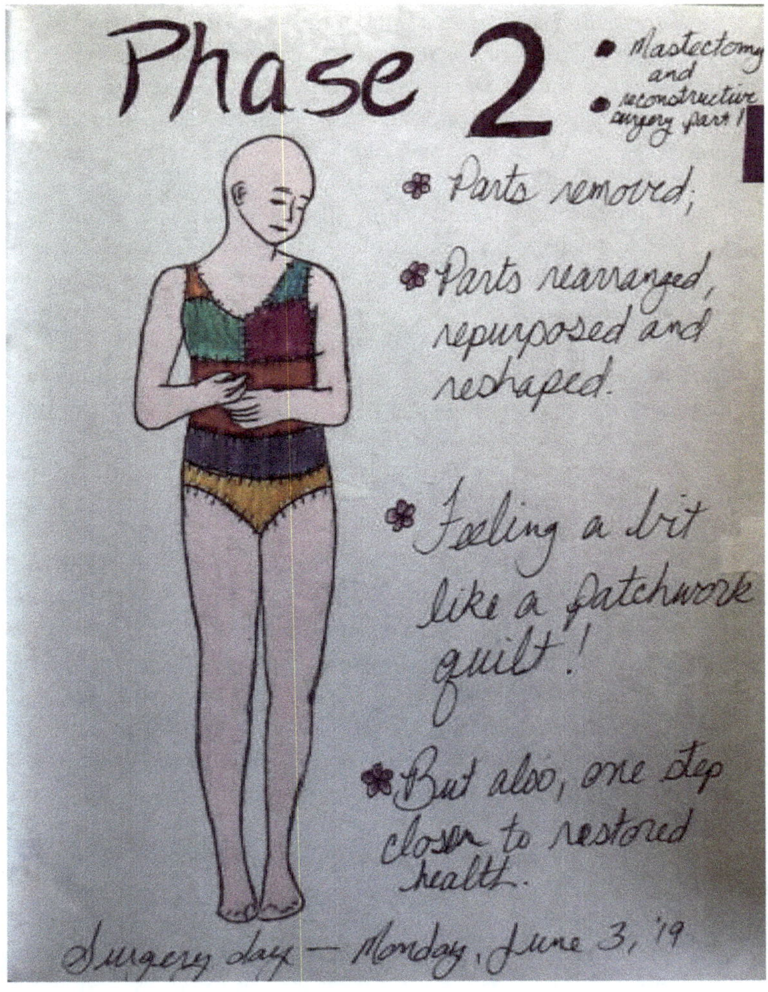

tissue confirm the absence of cancer. The former feeling of having been betrayed by my body is replaced with a feeling of gratefulness. I'm grateful to my medical team, but also to my body for enduring so much torture and overcoming tough odds. And, as a person of faith, I'm grateful to God for walking alongside me and answering my prayers.

I only have the weekend at home before going back in for a follow-up outpatient surgery called a "debridement" on the reconstructed breast. In a nutshell, an extra section of graft-ready skin from my belly was "banked" under the surface of the breast skin during the reconstruction process in case my own skin does not remain viable. In the outpatient procedure it is then either used or removed. In my case it is not needed, which makes this surgery last only a half hour, and makes for a much shorter recovery time. And 2 of the 4 drains are removed, which is an improvement.

It's a long 6-week recovery time. The remaining 2 drains are removed at my follow-up appointment after the first week, which makes me feel much more comfortable. I have quite a lot of restrictions during this time: sleeping only on my back, wearing surgical bras or compression athletic bras day and night, wearing compression underwear during the day, no repetitive motions, no lifting anything over 5 pounds at first then 10 pounds after the first 2 weeks, and limits to the range of motion of my left arm. All of this is tedious, but necessary. Surprisingly, the hardest restriction for me is sleeping on my back. I have always been a side-sleeper with a preference for my left side. This is a tough adjustment.

And there's one more big restriction: no immersion in a bath, hot tub, or pool. For the first time in our lives we happened to have bought a house with a pool. And it's summer. And I can't get in for 6 weeks! Sitting on the side with my legs in the water and occasionally splashing my arms and head is not a comparable experience.

I gain strength and stamina. I have a follow-up office visit with my cancer surgeon 3 weeks after surgery. She is pleased with my recovery and sets up an appointment for my initial consultation with the radiologist. I confess that I had hopes of skipping past the radiation phase since all tests are showing the cancer gone. However, the radiologist explains that micro-particles of cancer cells can be left behind that can later grow large enough to begin multiplying again. Plus, the one lymph node under my sternum which had previously shown signs of cancer can't be surgically removed. It will need radiation to be certain.

I had hoped to dodge this bullet. It seems that the Dark Entity of Cancer still hasn't completely parted ways with me on this journey. I have more sacrifices yet to make in order to gain my freedom. I've sacrificed my health, my hair, parts of my body, as well as special times with family. The proposed radiation schedule will also prevent me from going on 2 of my hoped-for annual summer vacation trips. Damn Cancer!

PHASE 3: RADIATION
7/19/19-8/30/19

July 2019

The month begins with continuation of my routine: continued infusions of Herseptin and Perjeta, my quarterly echo-cardiogram to check my heart, and my 6-week follow-up with my plastic surgeons. They lift all restrictions (I can't wait to get in the pool!!) and schedule an appointment to see me 8 weeks after radiation for discussion of my final surgery. At that time, I will have a right breast lift and reduction to make me symmetrical again, and will have any revisions necessary on the reconstructed breast.

Besides more physical freedom of movement, my head gains some freedom as well. My hair has begun growing back; just a little, but enough to begin going without hats and scarves. I know to expect it to grow back a different color and texture. My formerly thick, coarse, graying-red hair is coming in baby-soft and all white so far. The color will likely continue to change as time progresses. I'm also told that my formerly straight hair will likely be curly. It's too short right now to determine that. However, it definitely looks more like post-chemo shocked hair than an actual style. I'm not yet wearing this new look with confidence. I must be patient. I'm told it takes 12-18 months to return to what it used to be like. Sigh. Another whole year of my life.

I have the pre-radiation set-up scans and have 3 little freckle-sized spots tattooed on my torso for the purpose of aligning the machine to the same mark each time. Dang, those tiny tattoos hurt! It's done in the "stick-and-poke" method, making me say, "Ow, ow, ow, ow, ow, ow, ow!" Trust me, it was a much stronger word than "ow" inside my head. I'm really tired of being poked by needles.

My schedule is for 30 treatments of radiation, administered daily, Monday-Friday. The appointments are expected to be short, but always at the same time. I will check in at reception, go to the changing room to undress above the waist and put on a robe, wait to be called, then get escorted to the radiation room by a technician. Once a week I will end my session with an office visit with the radiologist, who will examine my skin and talk with me about any questions or concerns. Everyone I've met there is friendly, cheerful, and seems non-anxious. I'm glad, since I have enough anxiety about all of this for everyone.

Celebration Night number 3 is held at home. It's a wonderful day for a swim, so we have celebratory toasts in the pool! Then we grill out for dinner and enjoy a relaxing evening. Marking these moments has become very important to me. It helps me keep a positive attitude as I check off each milestone along the road.

My first treatment is on July 19. I come wearing a soft sports bra, soft shirt, and carrying the recommended pure aloe gel for application afterwards. I have fair skin that burns easily, so I plan to be very careful and diligent with skincare. Although they ran me through a "practice session" so I would have a feel for what to expect, I'm apprehensive. The technician brings me back, double-checks my information, and escorts me through a tremendously thick metal door with the radiation symbol on it. Having recently watched a documentary about the Chernobyl accident, that symbol is not reassuring.

Two other technicians are waiting in the room to help me get set up on the table under the big scary-looking equipment. Feeling self-conscious and a little embarrassed, I remove the robe from my bare upper body and climb up. They help position me in the form that was molded to my body in order to keep me in the same position,

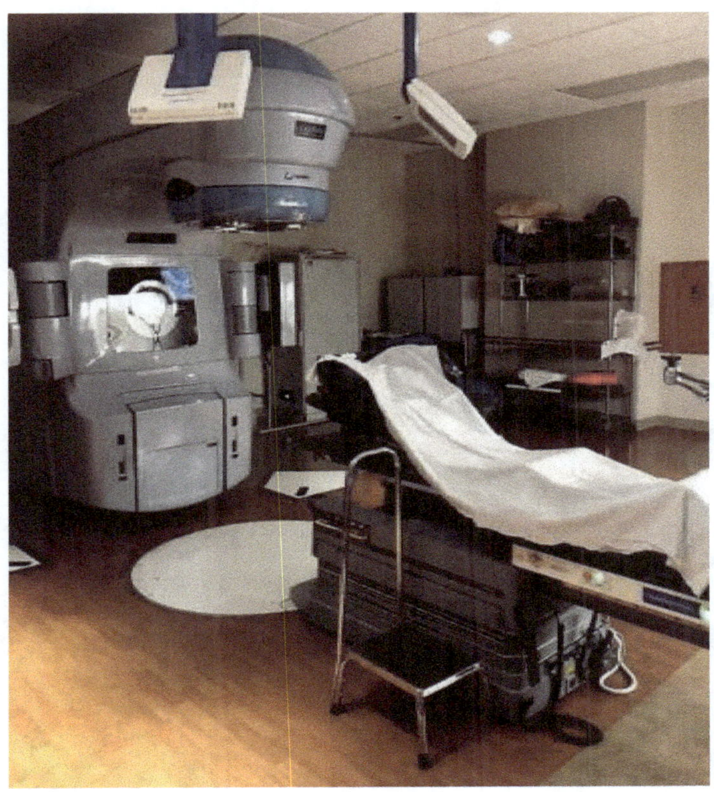

then align my 3 freckle-tattoos to the laser. Thankfully, they cover my right breast and arm with a warm blanket. As is usually the case in hospitals and treatment rooms, it is chilly in there.

And we begin. I have several zaps from different angles, each while holding my breath for 15-30 seconds to keep the chest wall lifted away from the heart. This is yet another treatment that has the potential of weakening my heart. The technicians are, of course,

safely on the other side of the huge metal door giving me instructions via intercom. I'm only under the scary machine for about 10 minutes, with each zap lasting only a very short time. It's over quickly. I don't feel tingling or anything at all during the radiation. But I know I will begin to get "sunburned" as this treatment progresses. I pray it will not be much worse than that.

Blessings continue to pour upon me from kind friends. Cards, supportive messages, and prayers are still cheering me along the path. I have even incorporated pieces of some of these cards into my art pieces as a way of carrying their love with me. A dear friend sent me a box filled with 15 little wrapped gifts and the promise of another box after that. She intends me to have a little surprise and joy to anticipate at the completion of each of my 30 treatments. What a loving and thoughtful gift! I'm deeply touched.

August 2019

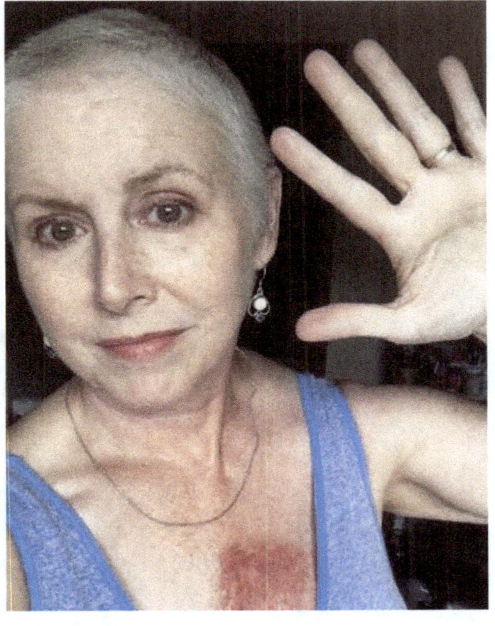

Visible signs of the radiation become evident by the halfway point: red, blotchy sunburned places that get progressively angrier each week. By the end of week 5 out of 6, my skin is deep red and very tender. I have been using aloe and the recommended ointment about 4 times a day, but now need a stronger prescription burn cream. With my skin in such bad shape, it takes every ounce of courage I can muster to climb up on that table for the final 5 treatments. The room is beginning to look like a torture chamber to me.

Martin comes along for the final radiation treatment to document the moment. I may not feel very pretty right now, but I smile my biggest smile when I get to ring the "graduation from treatment" bell. I feel free! A weight is lifted!

This calls for celebration. I know I still have the remainder of the year of the every-3-weeks infusions to finish, and I know I still have another surgery yet to come, but the worst is now behind me. We begin celebrating by going out for a special coffee where our daughter works. Raising our cups to the end of radiation, Martin talks about how he feels that during this journey nobody was truly able to take that walk with me. Cheer me and support me from the side of the road, certainly, but not truly able to be on the road. Nobody, that is, except Cancer. Together, Cancer and I were poisoned, cut apart, and burned. But only one of us survived.

Wow. I love this imagery that he has described and already have a vision for sketching it in my journal. Although in truth, I believe Cancer and I had one more companion on the road. My faith leads me to believe in a God that also endured the wilderness with me: One who was unseen, but never unfelt; One who held my hand when I was afraid or in tears; One who smiled when I smiled; One who went ahead of me, blazing the way through. And to that Holiness I owe my life.

The celebration of the milestone continues in the evening with a dinner out for our family. We get dressed up, take photos, and have champagne with our expensive dinner. It's worth every penny for me to share this moment with Martin, William, and Allison. The love and happiness glows all around us and I feel radiant!

PHASE 4: FINAL HURDLES
9/01/19-12/23/19

September 2019

Recovery from the radiation burns doesn't take as long as I feared. Energy returns rapidly. My skin looks horrid, peels away, then heals. Our bodies can be amazingly resilient. September feels like a welcome respite with no appointments marked in red on the calendar other than Herseptin and Perjeta infusions. I'm even able to schedule another trip down south to visit family members. It feels so good to escape my treatment plan for a brief bit!

October 2019

The month of October is full of check-list appointments. First, I see the radiologist, who bids me good luck and farewell. No need to see him unless any late-onset side effects creep into the picture (Fingers crossed!). Next, I have my follow-up with the cancer surgeon. She is very pleased with my response and recovery. She schedules my end-of-treatment diagnostic mammogram and will not need to see me for another 6 months. I end the month, a few days before my 59th birthday, with my post-radiation appointment with the plastic surgeon to discuss my final surgery.

Having reached the maximum out-of-pocket expenses with insurance costs, I'm hopeful that my final surgery can be squeezed into the final couple of months of the year. Unfortunately, the office is absolutely packed with other patients with the same hope. The nurse tells me that the schedule is fully booked all the way out. However, the surgeon tells me he feels there is a good chance they can work me in, since mine is an outpatient procedure. I receive a phone call the next day stating that mine was 1 of 40 cases they were trying to fit into the schedule and was given only 1 date as an option. I'll take it! But it's only 3 weeks away. Holy Cow!

November 2019

Thankfully, my primary care doctor, who also has a fully booked schedule, is able to work me into a time slot for my pre-op lab tests. My diagnostic mammogram was already scheduled, but is a mere 2 days before the surgery date. If any signs of cancer show up, all bets are off and we go back into treatment. I'm beyond relieved when I'm told that everything is fine. We're good to go.

Surgery is set for November 18. The procedure will take 2-3 hours. In addition to the reduction and lift of my right breast to match the size of my reconstructed breast, I will have some revision work done to the reconstructed side. Radiation altered it a bit, requiring some "fat grafting" to be done to fill in some indentations. So a little fat will be taken out of my inner thighs to fill in those areas. (Another silver lining perk!) Also, the ends of the hip-to-hip scar are pointed and need a little softening revision work.

Celebration Night number 4 occurs a couple of days prior to

surgery. We get dressed up and go out for a symphony orchestra performance at the beautiful Ohio Theater downtown. It's a lovely evening with good music and lots of smiles. I'm ready to begin the final trek towards the end of this arduous journey.

I'm not very nervous on the day of surgery. Our daughter has come along again to keep my husband company as he waits for me. It has been so helpful to me to have such wonderful family support. Too often, however, people don't realize that the care-givers need support as well. I'm glad she thought to be there for Martin.

I get to go home as soon as I'm fully awake in the recovery room and they have gone over the post-surgery care instructions. This time both arms have to remain in the T-Rex position for the first couple of weeks. That makes getting up and down a bit of a challenge. I'm extremely bruised on my chest, sides and inner thighs. Once again, I have to wear compression undergarments, sleep on my back, and endure a drain tube. Restrictions on lifting and range of motion are only for 4 weeks this time instead of 6.

In a week, just before Thanksgiving, I have a follow-up visit in which they remove the drain tube. Now we prepare for our annual trip to gather with Martin's family in the Chicago area. I'm feeling especially thankful this year. A year ago I was burdened with worry and uncertainty. Now I can be thankful to have more of life ahead of me. The finish line is in sight!

December 2019

I'm more excited than ever preparing for Christmas. Yet, as December 10 approaches on the calendar I'm finding my emotions all over the map, and end up crying most of the day. What the hell?! I would have thought the anniversary of the date of my diagnosis of cancer would have felt joyous and full of relief now that I'm almost finished with all of this. Instead, I have a recurrence of all the strong emotions I felt a year ago: fear, sadness, anger, desperation, and grief. It must be like a PTSD sort of response. I give my body and mind time to work through it and am able to get back to feeling grateful and hopeful.

Several days before Christmas I go back in to have sutures removed. I excitedly go straight from that appointment to buy bras. This may sound funny, but I haven't worn anything but clunky sports bras since my first surgery last June. It oddly feels like a treat to try on pretty, lacy things again! Merry Christmas to me!

I have my final IV infusion of Herseptin and Perjeta on December 23rd. I'm done! I made it! I endured the most torturous year I could have imagined following a most frightening diagnosis, and came out the other side a champion! Words cannot express what I feel. My body, which had betrayed me a year ago, has proven to be strong and resilient. I feel honestly and completely hopeful for the first time in the past year. This year I savor every moment during Christmas, but without the fear that it will be my last. I know that I will ring in the New Year with a hearty "good riddance" to 2019 and a joyous welcome to 2020.

January2020

So, what now? I switch my focus from treatment plan to healing and recovery. My hair, currently wavy and gray with hints of red highlights returning, now looks like an intentional short haircut. My eyelashes and brows have grown back, though shorter and less full. I will continue to see my oncologist and surgeon twice a year for the next 5 years. I have a hormone-blocking pill that I will take every day for that same amount of time, due to the estrogen positive nature of my cancer. I will have bone density scans twice more during that 5- year period

because of the possibility of bone loss from that pill. I will still have annual mammograms on my right breast. I will still keep up the heart-healthy exercise that has become routine for me. But somehow all of that seems almost anti-climactic after the year I have just endured.

Looking back, I know I have endured more than I ever thought myself capable. My body proved to be strong, able to withstand torture, and resilient in recovery. I learned patience, humility, and courage in the face of fear. My faith and love have grown deeper than ever before. And I cherish each day as a gift.

Normal, routine life can't be enough, can it? I feel the need to do more. I need to keep going with the artistic journey that I have begun. It's time to forge some new paths with my life. The journey ahead is still unknown territory for me, but, God willing, the dark and rocky wilderness terrain is behind. It's time to let the beautiful vista open up before me, leading into a new lush and fertile landscape. I am now like the phoenix who has risen from the ashes!

Onward into Life I go!

EPILOGUE

June 2020

Life can sometimes have seriously wicked ironic twists. Shortly into my new year of my new life, the world shut down amid the COVID-19 pandemic. New fears entered the picture for all of us. So much for the new lush landscape of existence I had hoped to be my next chapter. Life changed for everyone. Not fair!

The reservoir of my resilience and patience, discovered over the year of my cancer journey, has certainly been tested further. I have gained some perspective and have had time to reflect on where Life is taking me next. I have taken the time to write my story and create more artwork. Art saved my sanity over the last year and continues to be the way in which I wish to express my feelings and emotions as I go on. It has become a great part of my identity again.

So, once again, I ask "what now"? Nothing will be exactly the same as it was before. Many changes will be with us for at least another year. God, another whole year of life interrupted!

Still, my new lease on life must mean something. I want to share this newfound Hope with others. I want to share my expressions of thankfulness. Although fear is certainly still a part of the picture, I now know more of which I am capable. I know I can endure this hardship. I know survival is possible. I know some changes will not be permanent. I know I will not walk this road alone. Neither will you.

My hope is for the world to recover kinder and gentler than it was before. My prayer is for humanity to feel more connected to each other and to our planet. My part in the story is but a small one, but one that perhaps can bring a measure of comfort, hope, or inspiration to you. May your journey be filled with discoveries of deep resilience and love. Keep moving onward into Life!

A FURTHER WALK
THROUGH MY ART JOURNEY

The artwork that I created during my year of treatment and beyond has been very therapeutic and cathartic. Being creative and expressing myself through these pieces helped me to gain strength and to find a new sense of purpose during a time when I could have closed in and remain frightened and sad. Instead, I was able to find joy along the journey. Several of these artistic creations have included pieces of get-well cards that were sent to me by friends and family. The following pages include more of the journal sketches and paintings with descriptions.

Above is a 6x6" journal sketch (markers and get-well card piece) of resilience and renewal.

"The Peace of Creation" 5.5x6.5" journal sketch. This is a collage using my own nature photographs and color pencil illustration. It is a reminder to allow the Spirit to surround me with peace and calm.

"Straighten That Crown and Keep Going" 5x6" journal illustration using pieces of get-well cards. This reminds me to keep moving forward, no matter what comes.

"Holding On To Hope" 11x14" acrylic painting on canvas based on one of my smaller journal sketches. This painting reminds me that even a small light of hope can keep me going.

"Rainbow Self-Portrait" 5.75x5.5" batik and color pencil journal illustration. This reminds me that even though darkness surrounds me, there is light within that can shine through.

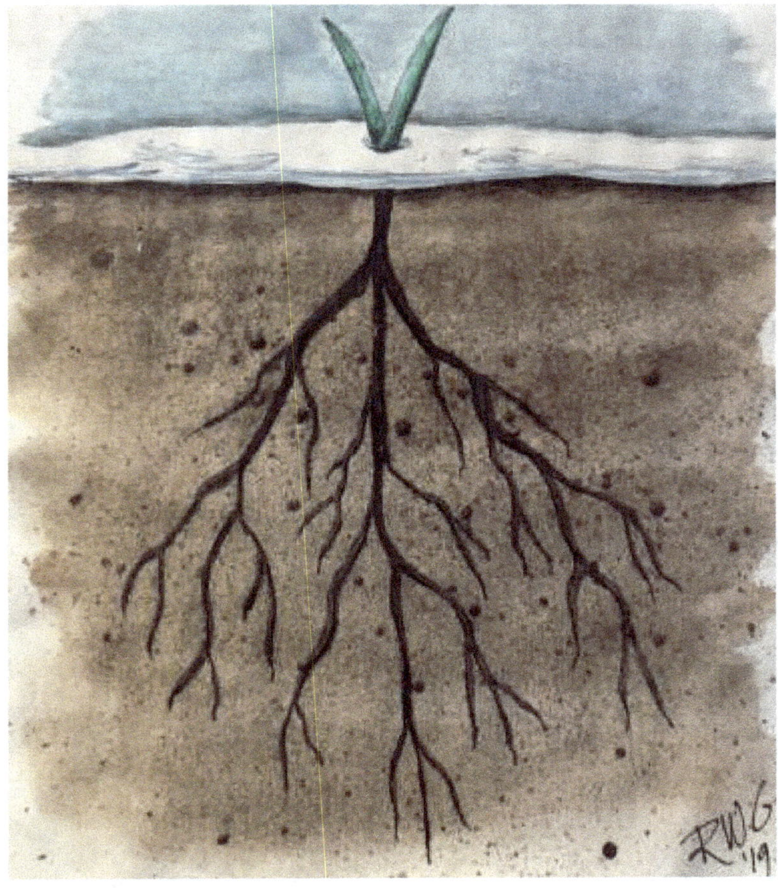

"Resilience" 6x7.25" watercolor journal illustration. This is a reminder that resilience can be found deep within us, like the roots of plants in winter.

"Peaceful Prayer" 11x14" mixed media acrylic and torn paper painting on canvas. This image is a reminder to center myself in peaceful calm in order to lower my feelings of stress.

"Blossoming Soul" 6x7.25" journal illustration using pieces of get-well cards. This symbolizes my gratefulness for all who supported me on my journey

"True Friends" 5.5x5.25" color pencil journal sketch. This illustrates a toast to some of the dear friends who sustained me through my darkest moments and cheered me to the end.

"On the Road Toward Hope" 14x11" mixed media acrylic and material collage painting on canvas. This painting is based on my journal sketch that symbolizes being on the road with cancer, but following the Holy One toward new life and hope.

"Dragonfly" 5.5x6.5" journal illustration. This is a collage illustration using watercolor, ink, and a flower from a get-well card. It symbolizes change, transformation, adaptability, and healing.

"Shattered and Remade" 7x7" journal illustration using ink, watercolors, and pieces of get-well cards. It symbolizes the shattered pieces fused back together into a new and beautiful being.

"After the Storm" 5.5x6" journal illustration using my own nature photograph, ink, and color pencil. It illustrates that moment after a storm seems to have ended when we aren't completely sure that it's really over.

"My Year of Treatments" 12x16" acrylic and paper painting on canvas. This painting represents all of my medical appointments through the 4 phases of my treatments, each one written on a leaf.

"Hope Shines Forth" 11x14" acrylic painting on canvas. This painting symbolizes hope breaking through and shining a light from my brokenness.

"Love Transforms" 11x14" mixed media painting on canvas. This collage painting uses flowers, butterflies, and a bird from many of the get-well cards that were sent to me.

ABOUT THE AUTHOR

Ruth Wilgus Gehring lives in Columbus, Ohio with her husband Martin and their 3 cats. She graduated in 1982 from Maryville College with a BA in studio art. Since then, she has been an advertising graphic artist, a stay-at-home mom, and a preschool teacher. But artwork was always her first love and now holds the primary position in how she occupies her time. This is her first publication.